DRAGONS
OF THE DEEP

Written by **CARL WIELAND**

Illustrated by **DARRELL WISKUR**

M₃
Master
Books

First Printing: April 2005
Fifth Printing: December 2014

For information write:
Master Books®, P.O. Box 726, Green Forest, AR 72638
Master Books® is a division of the New Leaf Publishing Group, Inc.

ISBN: 978-0-89051-424-5
Library of Congress Catalog Card Number: 2004118183

Printed in China

DEDICATION
To my colleagues in creation ministry with the courage
to take a stand rather than "go with the flow."

ACKNOWLEDGMENTS
My grateful thanks to Tim Dudley for igniting my passion for
this project, with its tremendous scope for communicating so
many aspects of a biblical worldview to young and old. Also to
Kym Holwerda for her diligence in checking the text.

Master Books®
A Division of New Leaf Publishing Group
www.masterbooks.net

TABLE of CONTENTS

The Dragons in the Sea

Mention huge, awesome creatures roaming our planet and most people think of dinosaurs that lived mostly on the land. Fearsome giants like *T. rex* and plant-eating earth-shakers like *Brachiosaurus* are gone now, recalled only in the dragon stories of many cultures. Since the Curse on all of creation (Genesis 3) brought in death, disease, and bloodshed to a once-perfect world, many types of creatures are no longer with us.

The bones of such extinct animals (and sometimes bits of flesh and skin), along with the remains of many creatures that are still with us today, are found buried and preserved in huge layers of rock. These layers were once mud or sand, laid down all over the earth by massive water action (Genesis 6–9). The preserved remains are known as fossils.

The fossils also tell us that some of the most spectacular monsters in all of creation were designed to live beneath the waves. Moviegoers shuddered by the millions at the rampaging great white shark portrayed in *Jaws*. Few would have been aware that it could have been swallowed whole by another type of shark, of truly monstrous proportions, that once also lived in our oceans.

Many people are familiar with the marine reptiles called plesiosaurs and ichthyosaurs. Very few, however, have heard of the mighty *Kronosaurus*, which could have had the average-sized ichthyosaur for breakfast. Nor do they know much about *Mosasaurus* and other sea monsters featured in this book — most extinct, but some still living.

Monsters in the Bible

The Bible mentions a creature called "Behemoth." This was obviously alive at the time the Book of Job, with its majestic poetic language, was written. From the description in Job chapter 40, it was the largest land-dwelling, grass-eating creature God ever made. The description of its tail moving "like a cedar tree" has perplexed many commentators who realize that it cannot be an elephant or hippo. Behemoth sounds much like one of the big land-dwelling dinosaurs.

The Scripture then talks of "Leviathan" (still used today to refer to a sea monster). This is clearly a marine animal, with fearsome teeth, and armor-plated scales that shrug off spears and arrows. It is large and powerful, making the notion of its capture by humans appear ridiculous as the sea "boils" or "churns" in its wake.

Dolichorhynchops

The references to its flaming breath and smoking nostrils may simply be poetic descriptions of its fearsomeness. However, these references are intriguingly consistent with the recurring, ancient accounts of some dragons having similar features. The living bombardier beetle mixes highly reactive chemicals together to fire boiling hot blasts at its enemies. There is no biological reason why some creatures may not have had (for defensive or display purposes) similar built-in "chemistry sets" enabling heat and smoke to be produced.

The incredible range of God's creation included many awe-inspiring sea monsters, a few of which are still alive today. One of the extinct ones featured in this book may well have been the Leviathan of Job. All of them will open up a whole new dimension of fascination and wonder as we contemplate these real "dragons of the sea."

MOSASAURUS

A magnificent predator, *Mosasaurus* was a sea-dwelling reptile that has been called the marine equivalent of *Tyrannosaurus rex* — only much bigger. Known today only from fossils, mosasaurs (this is the name given to the whole group that includes *Mosasaurus*) came in a wide range of sizes. Some were truly huge. From their bones, it is estimated that some could have been up to 50 feet (15 m) in length, more than a four-story building on its side. If so, that would make such a creature the biggest predatory carnivore (flesh-eater) the world has ever known.

The bones of mosasaurs have been found on every continent of the world, including Antarctica. They had long, snake-like bodies, and would have used their long, sinewy tails to propel themselves powerfully through the water with a side-to-side motion. These animals probably could not swim fast for very long distances, but would have been able to ambush their prey by

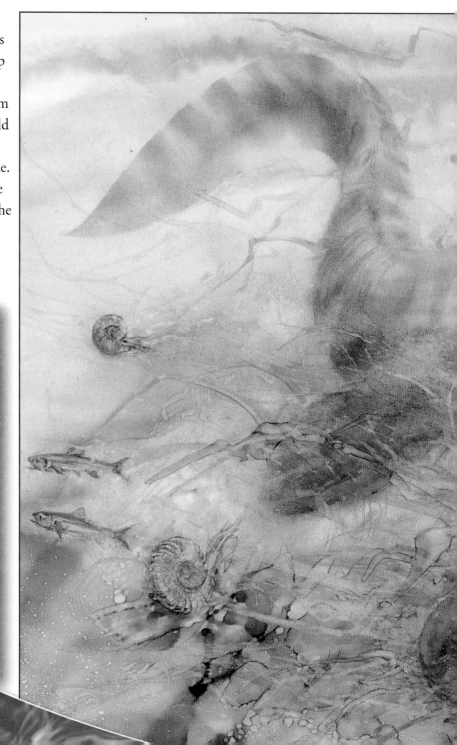

Fast Facts

- Meaning of name: "Meuse River reptile"
- Length: up to 50 feet (15 m)
- Weight: 8–10 tons
- "Discovered": somewhere between 1766 and 1774
- Location of fossils: worldwide
- Nifty fact: The lower jaw of *Mosasaurus* was loosely hinged and moveable on each side. Just like some living snakes, this loose joint allowed it to swallow large prey.

surprising them, and outswimming them in a burst over a short distance. Their broad, paddle-like legs were primarily useful for steering.

They had a long, pointed head with powerful jaws containing many long, sharp teeth. Although some of the other "sea dragons" in this book come close to the biggest mosasaurs in size — and some could have been fiercer, even possibly stronger — it seems that mosasaurs, so far, have the size record for such marine hunters.

Samples of fossilized skin have been found, showing that some mosasaurs had large dermal plates, called "scutes," covering their skin. It is not clear, though, whether these extended farther than the neck or throat.

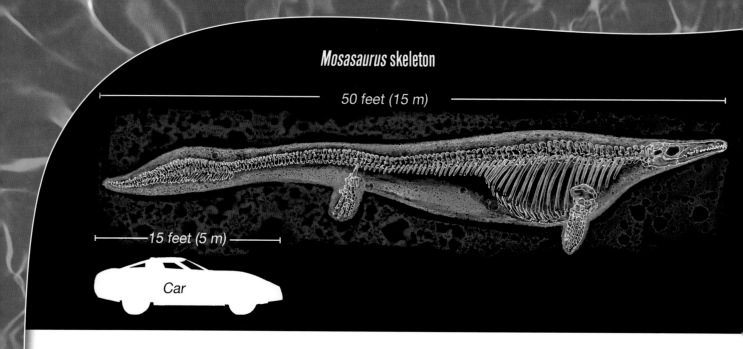

Mosasaurus skeleton

50 feet (15 m)

15 feet (5 m)

Car

However, other mosasaur specimens have revealed small scales, similar to the pattern of a rattlesnake, covering the whole body.

The name "mosasaur" comes from the River Meuse (or Maas) in Holland where the first fossil of this creature was found in the late 1700s. Another 70 years or so passed before scientists began to describe dinosaurs (the land creatures) whose fossils had been reconstructed. As research papers and textbooks began to make knowledge of the dinosaurs widespread, marine reptiles like mosasaurs were being discovered in increasing numbers, so they became associated in the public mind with an "age of dinosaurs."

Throughout this book the Fast Facts sections show the dates that the fossils of each creature (or the creature itself) were discovered. These dates are shown in quotation marks because for extinct creatures, it might actually be better

termed "rediscovered." People were present from the beginning of creation (Mark 10:6), so ancient people probably knew about the existence of such impressive creatures in the sea, especially when many of them, like mosasaurs, needed to come to the surface regularly to breathe air. Even the ones that are not extinct would have been seen by fishermen and native peoples long before they were officially "discovered" by European explorers or scientists.

It is true that so far no one has found a fossil of a person together with the fossil of a mosasaur. Does that mean that mosasaurs lived millions of years ago before there were people? Hardly; the fish called coelacanths are known from their fossils, which are found in the same layers as dinosaurs, mosasaurs, and other reptiles. No human (or whale) fossils have been found in the same rocks together with coelacanths. Yet coelacanths definitely lived with humans and whales. How do we know? Because several populations of coelacanths have been found to be living today, on the same earth as people, whales, and many other creatures that we never find with them in the fossil record.

Coelacanth

People often think of the many types of marine reptiles, like mosasaurs, ichthyosaurs, and the like, as dinosaurs, but this is not so, strictly speaking. The same is true for the extinct flying reptiles, called pterosaurs. Dinosaurs, which spent a lot of their time on land, are placed in a separate major grouping from both marine reptiles and flying reptiles. So marine reptiles cannot be called "sea dinosaurs."

MEGALODON

Sleek, quick, massive, and with somewhere around 200 razor-sharp teeth, *Carcharocles megalodon* was one of the most feared predators ever to roam the seas. At 50 feet (15 m) in length or more, it was longer than a school bus. Its dorsal fin (the one on its back) would have stood about six feet above the water. A tooth from *megalodon* could be larger than a man's hand. With massive jaws that could open to seven feet, it could have easily devoured a small fishing boat in one bite.

Just like any other creature that is thought to have died out since its kind was first created, what we think we know about *megalodon* is based on the fossils that remain, but *megalodon* was a member of the shark family, and sharks' skeletons are composed of cartilage, not bone. Even if suddenly trapped and buried in sediment, as happened to billions of creatures worldwide during Noah's flood, the cartilage is much more likely to rot away than be

Fast Facts

- Meaning of name: "giant tooth"
- Length: 40 to 50 feet (12–15 m) or more.
- Weight: 20 tons or more
- "Discovered": 1843
- Location of fossils: worldwide
- Nifty Fact: With jaws that could open to 7 feet (2 m), *megalodon* could swallow a large great white shark whole!

preserved. A few fossilized pieces of *megalodon* skeletons have been found, but most of our speculations about this giant fish are based on the many teeth found. Being composed of a bone-like material and coated with enamel, they are more likely to be preserved.

These huge teeth resemble those of the present-day great white shark, only two-and-a-half to three times larger. So scientists think this creature must have been like a great white shark times three! The tooth marks found in some fossilized bones of whales show jaw patterns which match the dimensions worked out for *megalodon*. In fact, whales were probably a favorite food. Sharks eat about two percent of their body weight each day. Even at a low estimate of 20 tons for

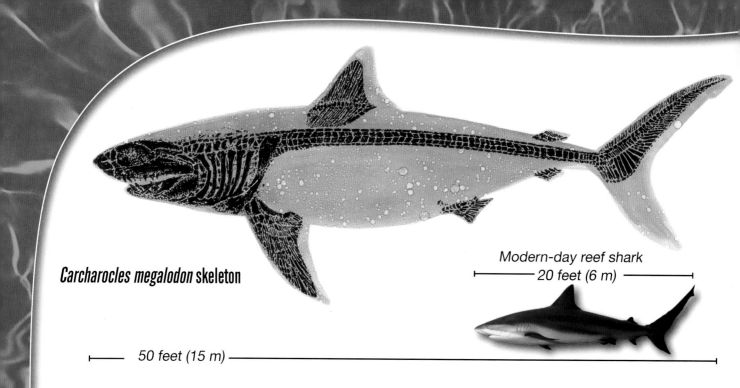

Carcharocles megalodon skeleton

Modern-day reef shark
|— 20 feet (6 m) —|

|— 50 feet (15 m) ————————————————————|

megalodon's weight, it would have had to eat about 800 pounds of food a day, and some scientists speculate that an adult *megalodon* may have weighed up to 65 tons! It's no wonder that these creatures chomped on some types of whales.

Sharks have three to five rows of razor-sharp teeth. They do not chew their food like humans do. Instead, they simply chomp and gulp, swallowing the meat in huge chunks. Their teeth often break off or fall out with all of that chomping, but it doesn't matter to the shark. A tooth from the next row will take the place of the missing tooth within 24 hours. A shark may go through 20,000 teeth in an average lifetime. That's why sharks' teeth are found in great numbers on the sea floor and beaches. So *megalodon* teeth, found all over the world, have probably mostly fallen out of a living shark, rather than being fossilized with it.

Some of these teeth appear remarkably fresh, which has led people to speculate that *megalodon* may not be extinct yet. In 1918, a group of lobster fishermen in Port Stephens, Australia, reported an encounter with "an immense shark of almost unbelievable proportions" that devastated their catch and left them in a state of shock. *Megalodon* would not be the first creature, known from its fossils and believed to be extinct, to have later been discovered still living in the sea's massive depths.

While doing some maintenance on the dredge arm of the *Eagle I* (pictured), crewmember Jeff Sinclair discovered the *megalodon* tooth shown on the opposite page. The ship had last worked near the shoreline of Louisiana. The *Eagle I* is a dredging ship, a special vessel designed to "clean out" shipping channels throughout the world.

1"

A tooth from a modern-day great white shark

4"

A tooth from a *megalodon* shark
(actual size)

Was megalodon simply a giant version of the great white? It is often given the same genus name, Carcharadon. But lately, due to some differences in the teeth, it is more often given its own genus, Carcharocles. However, this is controversial, because the larger the teeth of great whites, the more they resemble megalodon's. The two may well have belonged to the same Genesis kind.

KRONOSAURUS

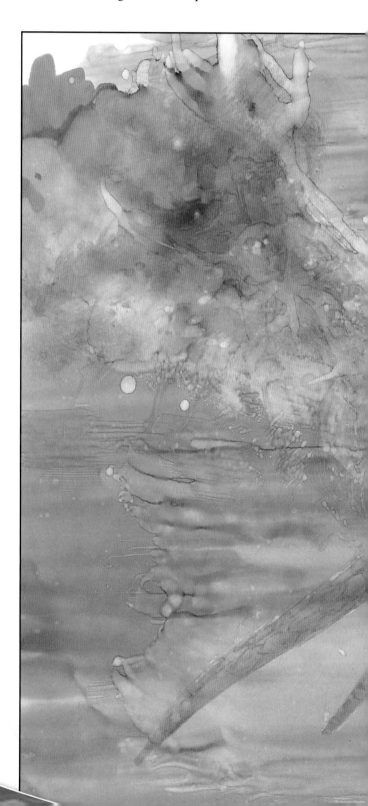

The "terror of the seas" is a term commonly used for this fearsome (but now almost certainly extinct) giant. The reputation may have been deserved, but recent studies have also raised doubts about some of the things that have long been believed about *Kronosaurus*, especially about how long it was, as we shall see. There is no doubt, though, that this mighty sea reptile had a huge skull with powerful jaws that combined the biting power of killer whales and crocodiles. Its back teeth were designed to crush even the toughest shells.

The most well-known specimen is mounted in the famous Harvard Museum. Judging from that spectacular display, *Kronosaurus* would have been around 50 feet (15 m) long. The specimen was unearthed in Queensland early last century, but it was badly eroded. The famous paleontologist (fossil expert) Alfred Romer helped put it together. He had to use a lot of imagination and plaster of Paris to fill in

Fast Facts

- Meaning of name: "time reptile"
- Length: up to 33 feet (10 m)—earlier estimates of 50 feet were due to a "padded" reconstruction
- Weight: 8 to 10 tons
- "Discovered": 1920s
- Location of fossils: Australia, South America
- Nifty fact: Fossilized plesiosaurs and turtles have been found within the abdominal cavity of *Kronosaurus* fossils.

"missing bits" — so much so that it earned the nickname "plasterosaurus" in some quarters.

Unfortunately, it appears that Romer went so far as to add as many as ten extra vertebrae (bony spine segments). So *Kronosaurus* may have only been about 30 feet (9 m) long after all, although still bulky and strong enough to attack and eat many a smaller plesiosaur.

It's easy to be confused when a short-necked creature like *Kronosaurus* is called a plesiosaur, because normally

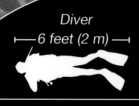

Diver
6 feet (2 m)

Kronosaurus skeleton

33 feet (10 m)

plesiosaurs are thought of as having very long necks. At other times, *Kronosaurus* is called a pliosaur, characterized by a short neck. Which is right? Actually both. *Kronosaurus* is classified within the very large group of marine reptiles known as *Plesiosauria*. This group includes both plesiosaurs (long necks) and pliosaurs (short necks).*

Although they may have many physical differences, all animals, including extinct marine reptiles, will have some physical traits in common with some of the other animals. These similar designs, which allow them to be classified within the same group, are claimed by evolutionists as proof of evolution.

However, these similarities simply show that all animals are the product of the same Designer. An example from the world of cars will make this clear. A few years ago, the Volkswagen Beetle car and the Porsche sports car each had rear engines. In both, the cylinders lay flat on their sides. Both engines were cooled by air and not water. These similarities were because they shared the same designer, Dr. Ferdinand Porsche. It was not because they evolved from some "joint ancestor."

Plesiosaur

Pliosaur

*To help you remember which is which, remember that the long necks have the longer suffix — "plesio" is longer than "plio."

Single vertebra of a dinosaur

In 1996, scientists hailed the discovery of a creature that was much like Kronosaurus, only 40 percent larger. They estimated it to be 65 feet (20 m) long and to weigh more than 50 tons. All of these estimates came from a single vertebra (bone from the spine). Eventually it was realized that it was most likely not from a marine reptile at all, but a large land-dwelling dinosaur.

XIPHACTINUS

than 800 pounds. Now that's a fish! The fillets from it would be enough to feed a family of four every night for more than a year!

As far as we know, no living *Xiphactinus* fish are around anymore. It is not classified in the same group as any living fish, but it would have looked much like a fish we know to be alive, called a tarpon, only much bigger. Judging by its size, its dagger-sharp three-inch-

You've probably hoped sometimes that a really big fish would latch onto the end of your fishing line. Not some shark or whale, but the sort of fish with bones and scales that you could imagine on the dinner plate. Well, *Xiphactinus* would have made all your dreams come true — or maybe turned them into nightmares if it had really struck at your hook. This wasn't just a large fish; it was monstrous — the biggest, most humungous bony fish that ever lived on this planet — and savage.

Reaching nearly 20 feet (6 m) or so in length, *Xiphactinus* was longer than your average family SUV. It could weigh more

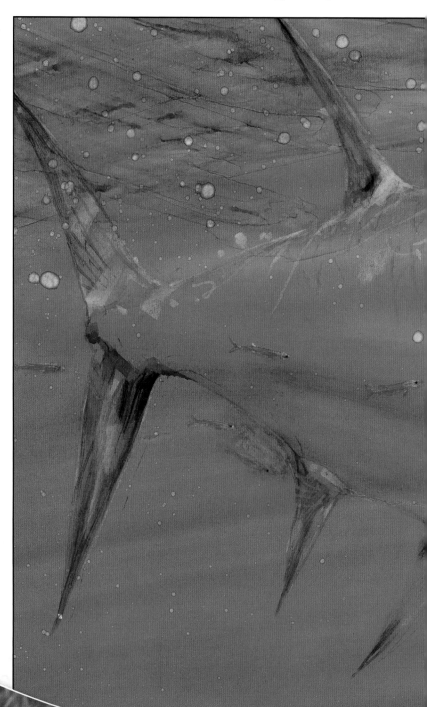

Fast Facts

- Meaning of name: "sword ray"
- Length: 19 feet (6 m) or more.
- Weight: 650 to 850 lbs (300–350 kg)
- "Discovered": 1870
- Location of fossils: United States
- Nifty fact: By swallowing its prey head first, *Xiphactinus* avoided the prey's fins from jamming its gullet and choking it on the way down.

long teeth, and its huge mouth, it would have been a ferocious and efficient predator.

The most famous fossil of *Xiphactinus* shows it with the fossil remains of another fish still inside it. That means it could swallow such fish whole, but it also shows that this particular fossil must have been buried rapidly. If it had been buried slowly, the fish inside would have rotted or been digested before the sediments (mud, sand, etc.) covered it up and fossilization began. In other words, both the burial and fossilization processes happened rapidly.

Rapid fossilization can also be deduced from the way in which billions of other fish fossils have been preserved; soft parts such as scales and fins would have rapidly fallen apart otherwise. This is consistent with the Bible's account of a massive watery catastrophe covering

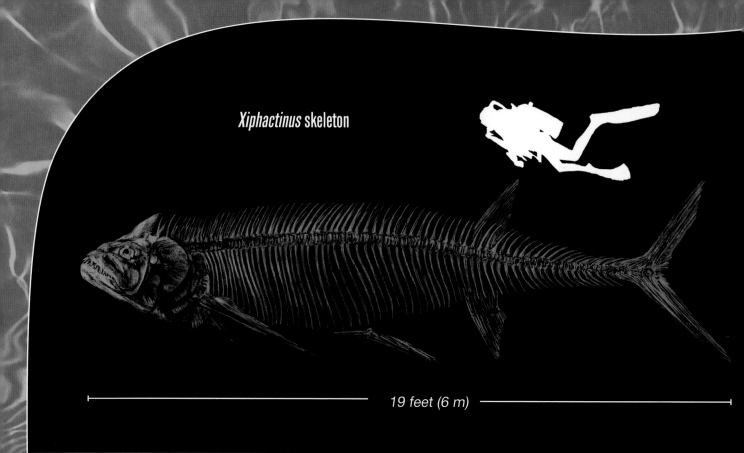

Xiphactinus skeleton

19 feet (6 m)

the whole globe for many months. It started with the breakup of the "fountains of the great deep" (Genesis 7:11) all over the globe, and huge earth movements would have occurred afterward, too. All of this gives ideal conditions for what are known as "turbidity currents" — massive underwater landslides. In modern times, these have been seen to happen after even minor earthquakes. They can carry thousands of cubic miles of sediment underwater at speeds of up to 60 mph (100 kph), so it's not surprising that they bury things in their path. No wonder we

see "billions of dead things buried in rock layers laid down by water all over the earth," and no wonder that most of these are marine creatures.

turbidity currents

Fossils, showing an animal in action, such as this fish eating another fish, give evidence of rapid burial and fossilization.

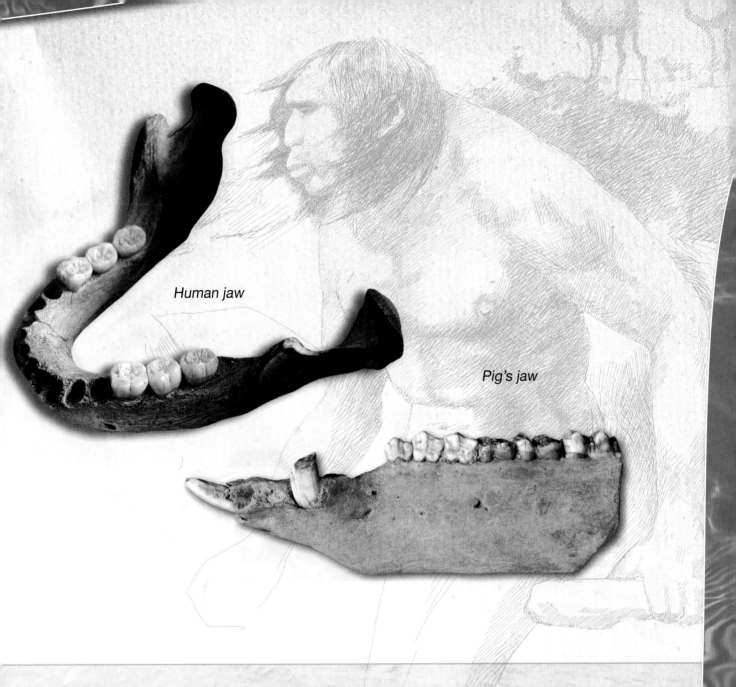

Human jaw

Pig's jaw

Professor Joseph Leidy was a brilliant U.S. naturalist of the 1800s, but he described and named *Xiphactinus audax* on the basis of nothing more than a 16-inch (41-cm) fragment of fin found in Kansas. It's no wonder that he got it quite wrong; he identified it as a giant catfish.

In the world of science, the urge to have the honor of being the first to "discover" a fossil species has sometimes led to exaggerated claims and reckless reconstructions based on very scanty evidence, even by those who should know better. "Nebraska Man" was described in detail as a new species of "ape-man/missing link" based on a single tooth found in western Nebraska. This later turned out to be a pig's tooth (notice the differences in the two types of teeth above). In that case, the fervor to "prove" that man evolved, and thus discredit the Bible, was a driving factor.

SHONISAURUS

This huge creature was for a long time the largest ichthyosaur — the name means "fish lizard" (or "fish reptile") — ever found. Most of the ichthyosaurs, now extinct, were similar to dolphins in size and shape. *Shonisaurus,* however, was right up there in the big league of massive sea creatures. Its huge body weighed as much as 30 or more automobiles together. Its skull alone was some 10 feet (3 m) long, and its entire body was longer than a schoolbus. A person would have looked bite-size next to one of these giant reptiles.

Ichthyosaurs ate things like fish, squid, and smaller sea creatures. Some of the dolphin-sized ichthyosaur fossils have been found with baby turtles in their stomachs.

All reptiles, like mammals, breathe air, even though they may live in water. So, just like turtles, whales, and dolphins do today, ichthyosaurs would have had to come up for air from time to time.

Most, but not all, reptiles lay eggs, which then hatch outside their bodies. In some, the eggs are

Fast Facts

- Meaning of name: "Shoshone Mountain reptile"
- Length: 50 feet (15 m) or more
- Weight: up to 40 tons
- "Discovered": 1869
- Location of fossils: western USA
- Nifty fact: *Shonisaurus* was adopted as the state fossil of Nevada, the state in which the fossils from which it was first described were found.

nurtured and hatch inside the mother's body, so they do give birth to live young, even though not quite in the same way as mammals. Ichthyosaurs, though reptiles, gave birth to live young in this way, too.

One of the most famous fossils in the world is a mother ichthyosaur, one of the smaller ones — about two meters long (shown on page 25). At the right, under the tail, is a baby ichthyosaur almost out of the birth canal — only its beak is still inside its mother! The general public still often associates fossil formation with slow and gradual burial by a gentle rain of sediment (like fine mud and sand particles) over a very long period of time.

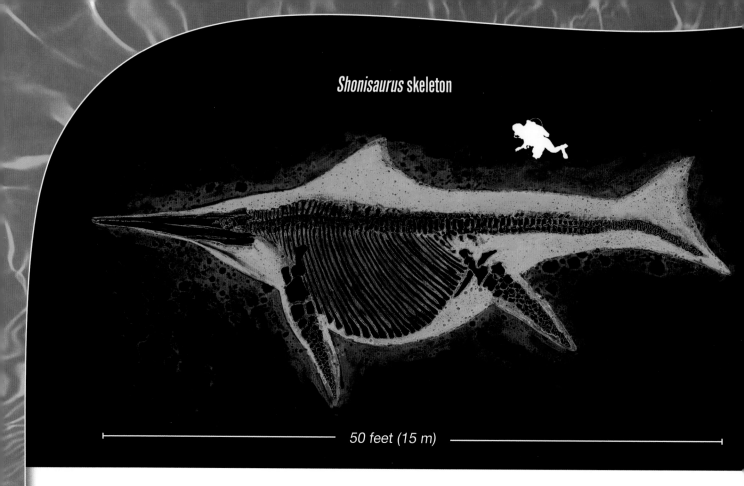

Shonisaurus skeleton

50 feet (15 m)

Obviously, even the most difficult labor would not last thousands of years while mother and baby were being slowly covered! This "frozen birth," and the beautiful way in which the whole fossil is preserved, show that it must have been the result of very rapid processes. It's not just that it was suddenly trapped and buried, either. The sediment would have had the right mix of minerals so as to harden fairly quickly. If not, oxygen, water, bacteria, and burrowing scavengers would have soon inflicted their damage on these animals' bodies. Evidence of rapid burial is what we would expect from the sorts of conditions that would have prevailed during a yearlong catastrophic Flood such as the Bible describes.

The location in which *Shonisaurus* fossils came to light is interesting, too. The Shoshone Mountains of Nevada are in the middle of a desert. Yet 36 *Shonisaurus* fossils were found together there, at an altitude of over 7,000 feet (2,134 m). Some have suggested that this unusual grouping could have been from a whole school of these massive reptiles beaching themselves, like some whales have been known to do. The problem with this explanation is that we know that such beached whales do not go on to form preserved fossil skeletons. Exposed on a beach, even their skeletons would just fall apart — unless they were catastrophically buried. Imagine what sort of catastrophe it would take to suddenly bury and cover 36 schoolbus-size creatures! Another evidence of rapid burial and massive watery action is the fact that the 36 shonisaurs were not found in haphazard directions, but all seemed to be more or less lined up in a north-south direction. This suggests that powerful water currents lined them up when they were washed into place by the catastrophe that preserved them. Since the Genesis flood covered the whole globe, it's no surprise that we find sea creatures in inland regions, too — including the tops of high mountains. Psalm 104:8, in the original Hebrew, talks of mountains rising up after the Flood as the waters retreated. These 36 dead shonisaurs would have been lifted up thousands of feet at the same time to their present location, over weeks, months, or perhaps a few years, but not millions of years.

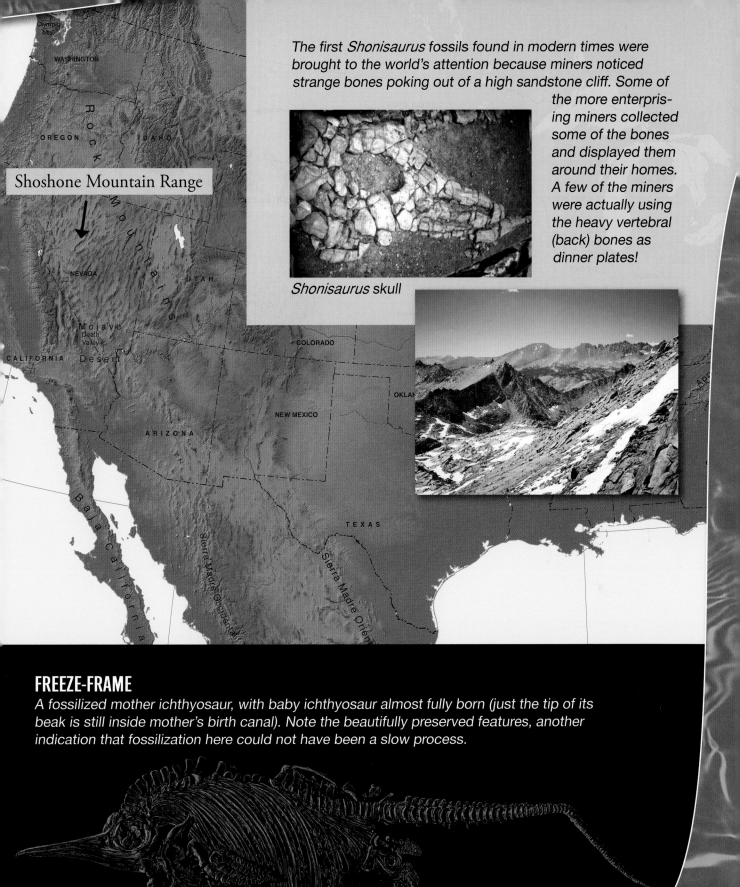

Shoshone Mountain Range

The first *Shonisaurus* fossils found in modern times were brought to the world's attention because miners noticed strange bones poking out of a high sandstone cliff. Some of the more enterprising miners collected some of the bones and displayed them around their homes. A few of the miners were actually using the heavy vertebral (back) bones as dinner plates!

Shonisaurus skull

FREEZE-FRAME

A fossilized mother ichthyosaur, with baby ichthyosaur almost fully born (just the tip of its beak is still inside mother's birth canal). Note the beautifully preserved features, another indication that fossilization here could not have been a slow process.

Kamikaze Ichthyosaur?

A sensational find

The complete preserved skull of an ichthyosaur was found in 1999 showing it was buried in an upright, nose-down position at 90 degrees to the rock layers when they were laid down. Unlike most fossils, it was not lying flat when buried, and it had not been flattened by the weight of sediment above it.

Found in the north of Switzerland, in Hauenstein, this famous specimen is now on display at the nearby Nature Museum of Olten. The layers which enclose it, according to the long-age, evolutionary interpretation, span an "age" of about one million years. However, no one can imagine an upright ichthyosaur head being buried slowly over such a long time while being preserved along its whole length. The obvious implication is that the "million years" is fanciful.

So how do long-agers deal with this? The evolutionist who discovered it, Dr. Achim Reisdorf, interprets the evidence by proposing that the creature died, then like a "kamikaze," plunged through the water fast enough that its head penetrated to its neck in the mud on the bottom.

Even if such a scenario were believable to this point, the "long ages" assigned to the layers create extra problems. One would have to believe that after at least one million years the sediments now surrounding the skull were all still soft enough for the ichthyosaur's complete head to sink right in, and yet right after that time they hardened quickly enough to beautifully preserve it.

These sorts of mental gymnastics highlight the fact that the tension between the Bible and many scientists is not about facts, but the way they are interpreted. If one abandons the long-age beliefs leading to the interpretation that the layers were laid down over a million-year time frame, the evidence can be understood in a straightforward way. The layers were laid down, and the ichthyosaur buried, as a result of rapid, catastrophic happenings.

Keeping an Eye on Things

All ichthyosaurs had relatively large eyes, which means they probably relied more on vision than smell or other senses to find their food. But one of them had extremely large eyes, even for an ichthyosaur. Its name was *Ophthalmosaurus*, which means "eye reptile." It was no longer than 16 feet (5 m), so it was dwarfed by the huge *Shonisaurus*.

The eye sockets in this creature were about 4 inches (10 cm) in diameter. Each of them occupied almost the whole depth of its side of the skull. The eyes of all ichthyosaurs were surrounded by a ring of bony plates which kept the soft eyeballs from collapsing under the outside pressure of the water. This ring also helped with focusing the vision, but the eyes in *Ophthalmosaurus* were strikingly larger. We don't know for sure why its eyes were so much bigger. Maybe it hunted at night, or in the deeper parts of the sea where less light penetrates. Being an air-breather would have limited the depth of its dives, of course. Even some seals, which also breathe air, have been known to dive over 5,000 feet (nearly a mile). The "deep diving" theory might be supported by the fact that its body was even more streamlined than most other ichthyosaurs.

Did *Ophthalmosaurus* have these more specialized features because it was created differently, a separate kind from other ichthyosaurs? Maybe. But it could also be that several types of ichthyosaurs descended from one original kind. That kind would have had the "instructions" (genetic information) to make a range of eye sizes, for instance. Those which were better suited to less well-lit environments would have survived in them when their fellow ichthyosaurs didn't. This sort of "survival of the fittest" (natural selection) is just common sense. Nothing new is created, but the less-suitable (for that situation) instructions are eliminated.

So natural selection can "fine-tune" a kind to its environment, using the information God had already programmed into its genes. It can't create anything new; it gets rid of things. In the same way, a mongrel dog kind can give rise to different types of dogs, each suited to differing "environments" (the breeder's requirements).

Even new species could have come about in this way, and would no longer breed with others in that group, but there would be nothing new created.

All of the instructions were already present in that original kind. So the *Ophthalmosaurus*, with its more specialized features, would actually have less information and less ability to vary further than the created kind that was its ancestor.

Temnodontosaurus ("cutting tooth reptile"), another ichthyosaur, actually had larger eyes than *Ophthalmosaurus*. In fact, at up to 10 inches across, they were the largest known eyes of any animal. But at 30 feet in length, and weighing up to ten tons it was so much bigger than *Opthalmosaurus* that its eye size seems less striking.

Ichthyosaurs used side-to-side movements of their fish-like tail, just like a shark or tuna does, to propel their bodies through the water. Plesiosaurs, on the other hand, relied mostly on their paddle-like flippers.

The name is a mouthful, but its other name, the "colossal squid," says it all.

Stories of a massive tentacled sea monster, capable of attacking a whale or a sailing ship, have circulated for many centuries. Norwegian sailors in the 11th century called it the *kraken*. The Disney movie *20,000 Leagues under the Sea* featured a famous battle between a giant squid and a submarine. The novel it was based on, the 1869 Jules Verne fiction classic, was inspired by such sailors' tales. These were long thought to be pure imagination, but whalers had for many years been finding what seemed like the remains of very large squid in the bellies of sperm whales. The bodies of some of those sperm whales carried scars which looked like they had been attacked by something with huge, hooked tentacles.

In recent years, complete specimens of *Architeuthis*, the giant squid, and more recently the

Fast Facts

- Meaning of name: "Middle-clawed squid"
- Length: 50 feet (15 m) or more
- Weight: Possibly up to 3/4 of a ton
- "Discovered": 1925 (described from parts in a whale)
- Location: deep Antarctic waters
- Nifty fact: *Mesonychoteuthis* has not one but two beaks, each shaped like a parrot's beak.

"much bigger and badder" *Mesonychoteuthis*, the colossal squid, have made it clear that the stories were well based in fact.

The ones recovered so far (one from a trawl net at more than a mile in depth) were not yet fully grown. It is clear from studying them (and the undigested parts, such as beaks, found inside sperm whales) that an adult *Mesonychoteuthis* is a formidable beast. It can grow to more than twice as long as a city bus, much longer than the longest sperm whale.

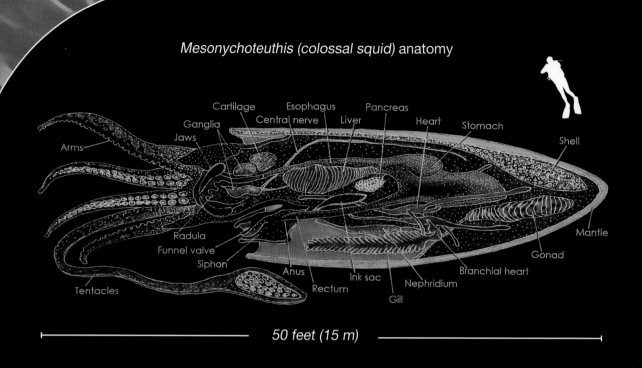

Mesonychoteuthis (colossal squid) anatomy

Cartilage
Esophagus
Pancreas
Ganglia
Central nerve
Liver
Heart
Stomach
Jaws
Shell
Arms

Radula
Funnel valve
Siphon
Anus
Ink sac
Nephridium
Branchial heart
Mantle
Gonad
Tentacles
Rectum
Gill

50 feet (15 m)

Its eyes, the largest in any living animal, are the size of dinner plates. It has eight arms and two tentacles. The middle of each arm has up to 25 tooth-like hooks (in addition to the usual suckers to ensure fish do not escape). Each tentacle also has on its "clubs" (the ends of the tentacles) 8–18 special hooks. These have razor-sharp edges and can rotate 360 degrees, like a circular saw. Contemplating this lethal array, one scientist said, "This animal . . . not only is colossal in size, but is going to be a phenomenal predator and something you are not going to want to meet in the water." Other scientists think that it would not usually attack humans, although its impressive weaponry would help it in defending itself against its main enemy, the hungry sperm whale. *Mesonychoteuthis* lives in very deep, freezing waters, mostly in Antarctica, so it is very unlikely that any of them would be seen by people. However, one of them was filmed, live, at the surface — attacking fish that grow as long as an average man.

The ocean's depths are very poorly explored. If the colossal squid had not been a favorite food of the whales hunted by people, we might still not know of its existence. We would think that it was pure legend. Who knows what "dragons of the sea" might lurk in the ocean's phenomenal depths? There may be creatures that no one has ever seen, or that are known so far only from fossils. There is much that is still to be discovered!

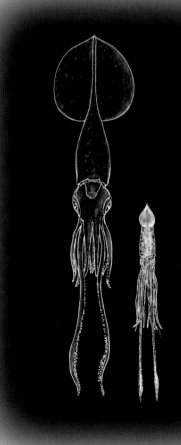

Colossal squid   Giant squid

The giant squid shown (right) was found in February of 1996 in waters off New Zealand.

Supersized *calamari* rings for dinner? Forget it. Such giant-size squid have a lot of very foul-smelling chemical ammonia in their bodies. It helps them to remain at the same buoyancy as the seawater around them. Having bad-tasting flesh also means that they are not so desirable to many predators, although it doesn't seem to bother the deep-diving sperm whales, which regularly feast on them.

STYXOSAURUS

In Greek mythology, "Styx" was the name of one of the five rivers winding its way through Hades. The name of this long-necked plesiosaur — now thought to be extinct — actually comes from the link between the mythological river and the fact that the first fossil was discovered at Hell's Creek, Kansas.

Styxosaurus is placed by scientists into the plesiosaur group called the elasmosaurs. About half of the entire length of elasmosaurs was taken up by their long, sinewy neck. Imagine such a marine reptile coming up to breathe, and seeing its snaky 20-foot (6-m) neck

(longer than three basketball players laid end to end) at the surface.

In the last chapter, we saw that the many sailors' tales of giant squid turned out to be mostly factual. There are also many stories (increasingly rare today) of sailors spotting long, sinewy "sea serpents," sometimes

Fast Facts

- Meaning of name: "Hell-river reptile"
- Length: up to 40 feet (13 m)
- Weight: up to 8 tons
- "Discovered": 1890
- Location of fossils: North America
- Nifty fact: Humans have 7 individual neck bones (vertebrae); *Styxosaurus* had nearly 10 times as many.

with humps. These could indicate that such long-necked reptiles may have been alive well after the Flood — even to recent times. This brings to mind the "monster sightings" at Loch Ness and some other deep bodies of water. The known hoaxes to one side, there appears to be a body of unexplained evidence at Loch Ness. If a large water-dwelling animal is responsible, it would not be surprising if it should turn out to be part of a population of still-living elasmosaurs.

The short-necked pliosaurs seem to have been built for short, powerful bursts of speed, but *Styxosaurus* may have been designed more for efficient cruising. One can imagine it sidling up to a school of fish, perhaps from beneath. Its relatively small head could be right in

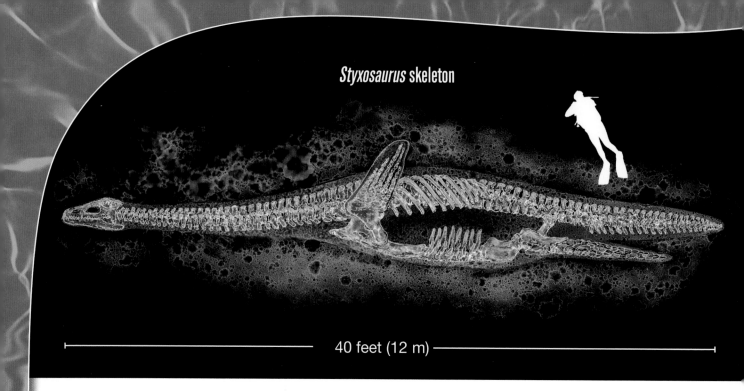

Styxosaurus skeleton

40 feet (12 m)

among the fish while its hefty body was still far enough below the school as to be out of sight.

In spite of its impressive length, *Styxosaurus* ate fish no longer than one or two feet long. Even though its teeth were long and sharp, they do not seem to have been designed for cutting and chewing. It probably used them just to seize and hold prey, which it then swallowed whole.

Plesiosaurs such as *Styxosaurus* have been found with many gastroliths ("stomach stones") inside their abdomens. These are real rocks that had to have been swallowed by the creature. When found today, they can often be highly polished from having been "tumbled" in this way.

Many types of birds and reptiles swallow stones that help them digest food by grinding it inside the stomach. Often hundreds, sometimes thousands, of these stones are found in association with plesiosaur remains. Some crocodiles swallow stones as ballast to counter their own buoyancy, causing them to sink. Then they vomit them up as required. This "regurgitation at will" would probably have been difficult for a creature with a neck this long. Even though the combined weight of the stones found in association with one plesiosaur is often well over a hundred pounds, this is still not much compared to the overall size of the animal. So they were probably not used as ballast, but to grind the plesiosaur's meals.

They would have helped break up food. Some plesiosaur gastroliths have been found to weigh more than three pounds. They are rounded and polished to varying degrees, depending on how long they have been in use.

Gastroliths

Elasmosaur skeleton

More careful studies of the bones of long-necked elasmosaurs like *Styxosaurus* have shown that many of the things believed about its behavior are wrong. For instance, it could not have cruised along while holding its neck high out of the water. It most certainly could not have moved its neck from side to side while doing so.

Interestingly, the famous Loch Ness photograph (right) which shows a long neck sticking high out of the water was a self-confessed fraud. The perpetrators were obviously influenced by the many pictures of plesiosaurs doing things that we know now to be impossible. However, other descriptions and photos of the alleged monster are more realistic of elasmosaur behavior.

The chilly waters of Loch Ness are as dark as the blackest coffee, so laden with *tannin* (from seams of peat) that visibility is limited to inches. Perhaps one day modern technology will help unravel the mystery of this immensely deep Scottish lake.

Alive and Well

Finding a plesiosaur alive today would be exciting, and would further reinforce the fact that the idea of an "age of reptiles" millions of years ago is mythological. Already, similar discoveries have been made involving other creatures. The "dinosaur fish," or coelacanth, known from its fossils found in rocks supposedly "millions of years old," was discovered living today. Similarly, the "dinosaur tree," the Wollemi pine, the fossils of which are found in the same rock layers as dinosaurs and marine reptiles, has been found living in Australia.

But sometimes what looks like evidence of a plesiosaur is not. The photo (below left) shows a carcass dredged up by Japanese fishermen off New Zealand in 1977. Because of what seemed to be a long neck leading to a small head, it was easy to think that this was a recently living plesiosaur.

The Wollemi pine, recently found alive and well in Australia

Careful research by scientists from the creation ministry Answers in Genesis, years later, confirmed that it was the partially decomposed carcass of a basking shark. (Even the original papers by Japanese scientists showed its backbone to be made of cartilage, like sharks, rather than bone, as plesiosaurs have.)

It was actually documented years ago that because of the way in which different parts of a basking shark rot faster than others, they tend to adopt a "pseudoplesiosaur" appearance in time, looking nothing like a shark.

The second photo, taken recently, shows an actual basking shark carcass washed up on the same New Zealand coast. Even more recently, news traveled across the Internet of a strange creature washed up on a Nova Scotia, Canada, beach. The pictures looked very much like these here. Despite once again generating "plesiosaur" excitement, DNA analysis confirmed it to be a decomposing basking shark.

Bizarre Creatures of the Deep

This newly discovered creature has yet to be named.

Blackdevil anglerfish

Fanfin anglerfish

HYDRODAMALIS

Many people know about the gentle vegetarian air-breathers called dugongs and manatees, but not nearly as many know that there were once monster versions of these lovable-looking, seaweed-grazing "cows of the sea." One of them grew longer than many types of plesiosaurs, and weighed as much as five or six automobiles.

Scientists place two species within the label *Hydrodamalis.* One of them *(H. cuestae)* is known only from its fossils. However, we know much more about the other (bigger) one, *Hydrodamalis gigas* (gentle water giant), because it was observed in action before it became extinct. It is commonly known as Steller's Sea Cow, named after Wilhelm Steller, a doctor and naturalist. Steller was on board the ship of the famous Danish explorer Vitus Bering, after whom the Bering Strait is named. This is the narrow body of water that now separates Siberia from Alaska. On its southern end, it opens into the Bering Sea. This gentle giant once thrived in the shallow waters surrounding several islands in this chilly sea.

Fast Facts

- Meaning of name: "water-gentle"
- Length: 25 feet (8 m) or more
- Weight: 10 tons or more
- "Discovered": 1741 (alive)
- Location of fossils: Japan, United States
- Nifty fact: The skin of *Hydrodamalis* was covered by a thick, black, bark-like layer that would have protected it from being injured on the rocks while it fed in shallow waters.

In 1741, Bering's crew was shipwrecked on one of the islands in the sea that now bears his name. Herds of these gigantic sea cows were everywhere around them, feeding on algae, soft kelp, and sea grasses. Steller had months to observe and record many details about this peaceful creature with its massive body and relatively tiny head. Lacking teeth, it ground its food between two deeply grooved plates in its jaws. These were made from keratin, like fingernails and hair. Its whale-like tail fluke was used in swimming. While feeding in the shallows, it pulled itself along with its stubby forelimbs, as if "walking."

The slow-moving *Hydrodamalis* seemed unafraid of people, and would ignore boats that came right up to it. Steller wondered: was this because it couldn't hear the boats? Its ear openings to the outside were only the size of a pea, but it was later shown to have had very large ear bones inside, so it probably could hear very well.

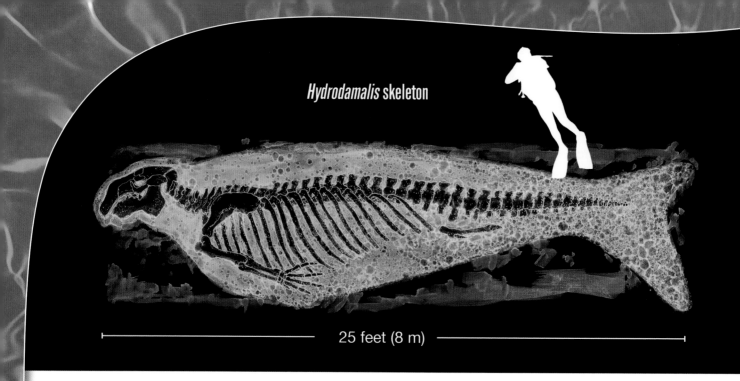

Hydrodamalis skeleton

25 feet (8 m)

With all that fresh meat floating around them, one would think that Bering's crew would have rapidly engaged in effortless hunting, but in fact, it was some nine months before necessity drove them to kill their first *Hydrodamalis*.

Perhaps it was the appeal of its gentle, lumbering passivity that made the sailors take so long before they hunted such an easy target. Sadly, though, others were not so inclined. As soon as the word got out, ships started to arrive to slaughter it for its meat (tasting like veal), fat, and skin. Within only 27 years of being described, it had vanished forever from the face of the earth. If not

for Steller's descriptions, a few skeletons, and bits of skin in museums, one might think that it was just an imaginary creature.

THE LIVING MANATEE Today's manatees and dugongs could have descended from the same created kind as *Hydrodamalis*. The "program" in a population of living things can contain an enormous amount of variation potential—within limits. However, the changes that lead to this "splitting up" into different species, often driven by natural selection, are downhill. One could not take a manatee today and breed a *Hydrodamalis*, no matter how much time was available. (Some of the information from the ancestral kind, which is present in *Hydrodamalis*, is not in the manatee.)

Asia

Migration Route

Did you know that the Bering Strait was once dry land connecting Asia and North America? During the great Ice Age caused by the drastically disrupted conditions after the Flood, people and animals migrating from the Ararat region could walk across it. The warmer temperature of the oceans from the massive global underground activity (Genesis 7:11) meant that much more water was evaporating into the atmosphere. This evaporated water fell again as ice and snow in the northern and southern parts of the earth.

Before long, huge glacial ice sheets formed on the land. Billions of cubic miles of water were removed from the oceans in this way and, for several centuries, were locked up on the land in frozen form. This means that during the Ice Age, the sea level everywhere was hundreds of feet lower than it is now.

North America

SARCOSUCHUS

Researchers were excited when a fossil of this monster crocodile was unearthed in what is now the Sahara Desert. The "super croc" was as long as a school bus, and would have weighed up to eight tons when alive.

The biggest crocodile around today is the feared saltwater crocodile that lives in northern Australia. These "salties" live in or near the mouths of rivers, but they are often found far out to sea as well. Fearsome predators that ambush their prey, they have taken quite a number of human lives. Even in captivity, these crocodiles have been known to kill or maim their keepers.

However, *Sarcosuchus* was twice as long as the biggest "saltie" and much, much bigger and stronger. Its jaws alone were around six feet (nearly two meters) long, and incredibly powerful. The much smaller saltwater crocodile is capable of dragging huge buffalo underwater when they come to the river's edge to drink. *Sarcosuchus* could have easily done this to even much larger creatures, such as some of the medium-sized dinosaurs.

Could *Sarcosuchus* have been the awesome Leviathan of the Bible? We said on page 5 that

Fast Facts

- Meaning of name: "flesh (-eating) crocodile"
- Length: up to 40 feet (12 m)
- Weight: up to 8 tons "Discovered": 1964
- Location of fossils: Africa
- Nifty fact: The eye sockets of *Sarcosuchus* were tilted upward, which would have helped it to watch its prey on the shore while keeping its body concealed under water.

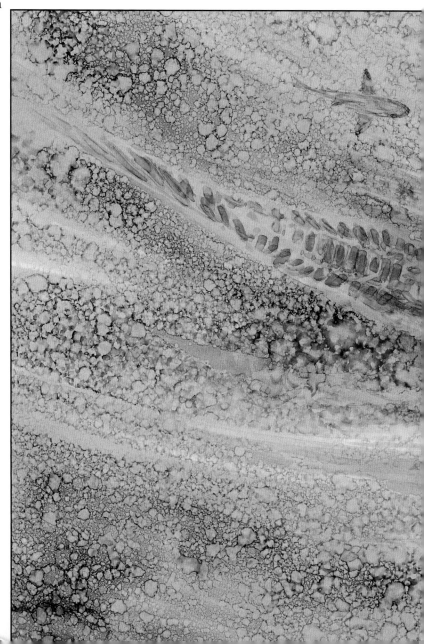

Leviathan was described as being virtually impossible for people to capture or kill with spears and arrows. This is quite possible, though difficult, with even the biggest crocs today, but the size and strength of *Sarcosuchus* puts it in a vastly different league. Job 41:14 says of Leviathan: "Who dares open the doors of his mouth, ringed about with his fearsome teeth?" The jaws of *Sarcosuchus* were lined with more than 100 teeth which one researcher described as "railroad spikes."

Many of the bony armor-plating scales of *Sarchosuchus*, called "scutes," have been found. These closely overlapping shields covered it from head to tail. Each one is around a foot long! Verse 15 says of Leviathan: "His back has rows of shields tightly sealed together." It truly would have been laughable to contemplate people killing such an armored beast with spears or arrows, as the Bible says.

Verse 30 reads: "His undersides are jagged potsherds, leaving a trail in the mud like a threshing sledge." It's hard to imagine a sea-dwelling beast like *Mosasaurus* spending time in the mud, but this fits an amphibious creature like this giant crocodile.

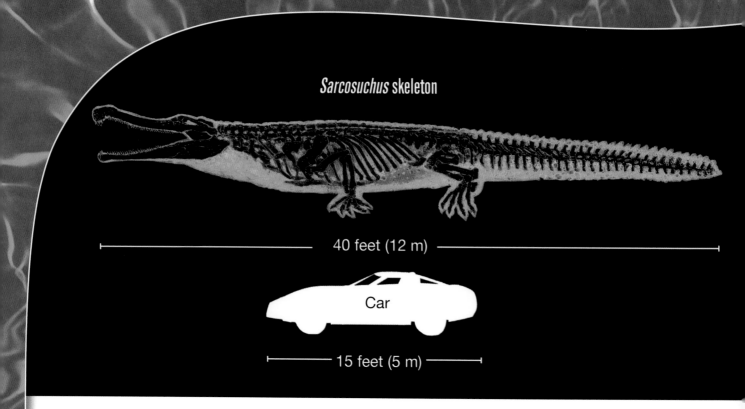

Sarcosuchus skeleton

40 feet (12 m)

Car

15 feet (5 m)

Intriguingly, the snout of *Sarcosuchus* contains a round, bony protrusion in its tip which housed a large, bowl-shaped cavity called a "bulla." Scientists are unsure of its function. Was it used for making sounds? Or could it have had something to do with the production and mixing of certain chemicals to give off heat and smoke, just as in the Bible's description? We may never know, but this speculation is well within the realms of biological possibility.

A crocodile in the desert?

It is widely accepted that what is now the Sahara Desert was once a vast, lush region. Satellite photos from outer space reveal the paths of the rivers that once flowed. While the greater evaporation from the warmer oceans after the Flood (see previous section) was causing ice sheets to build up in the north and south of our planet, elsewhere it was generating much rain. After hundreds of years, when the oceans had cooled off to their present balance with the air, the rainfall dropped. Once-lush areas like the Sahara and central Australia rapidly dried up. As the climate changed, rainforest vegetation disappeared, except in small

protected areas watered by springs, such as Australia's Palm Valley.

The *Sarcosuchus* that was found in the Sahara probably lived near the mouth of a large river after the Flood, its fossil the result of a local upheaval. There would have been many of these in the early centuries after this global catastrophe, as the earth was settling down. At any rate, if *Sarcosuchus* was the Leviathan of the Bible, it must have survived the Flood; the firsthand account of it in the Book of Job was written after the Flood.

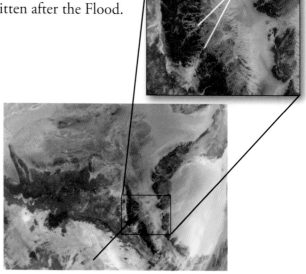

The ancient riverbeds are clearly visible in the Acacus-Amsak region of the Sahara Desert in this satellite photo.

Paleontologists said on October 24, 2001, that they discovered the fossilized remains of a gargantuan cousin of modern crocodiles during digs in the Tenere Desert of Niger in North Africa. The *Sarcosuchus imperator* (meaning "flesh crocodile emperor") dwarfs a 50-centimeter (20-inch) adult skull of the living Orinoco crocodile *(Crocodylus intermedius)* in this undated illustration below.

We know from a fossil skull almost as big as that of *Sarcosuchus* that there was once another type of giant crocodile. Although researchers think it was not as heavy as *Sarcosuchus*, it may actually have been even longer! It has been named *Deinosuchus* (terrible crocodile).

RHINCODON

magine 24 pickup trucks piled on top of one another. That's how heavy this huge creature is! Imagine the most monstrous *megalodon* shark (already longer than a bus) that ever lived. Now put the longest known *Rhincodon* next to it. *Rhincodon* would be 15 feet longer than *megalodon!* No wonder it's more commonly called "whale shark." But in spite of its massive size, it's not a whale. It's a fish — a shark — that breathes through gills. In fact, it's the biggest fish alive today. Its back is covered with a very distinctive and unusual pattern.

An unsuspecting diver who glanced over her shoulder and saw one of these giant sharks bearing down on her couldn't be blamed for being terrified. Actually, she would be just as safe as if she were in the sea before the Fall when all animals were *herbivores* (plant eaters) (Genesis 1:30). This shark is harmless to humans and

Fast Facts

- Meaning of name: "snout tooth"
- Length: up to 65 feet (20 m)
- Weight: up to 15 tons
- "Discovered": 1828
- Found: in all tropical/warm-temperate seas (except the Mediterranean)
- Nifty fact: *Rhincodon* can live up to 150 years.

other creatures of the type the Bible calls *nephesh chayyah* (living or "soulish" creatures, capable of suffering and pain). Seals, for instance, can frolic around the whale shark in peace and safety. Instead of eating such animals, it feeds on very small (mostly microscopic) plants and animals which it filters from sea water.

There are many other sea creatures that feed in this way, including some whales. They are all known as "filter feeders." Most of them use their forward swimming motion to "scoop up" enough of the nutrition-rich seawater to be able to get sufficient food. In contrast, *Rhincodon* usually feeds standing

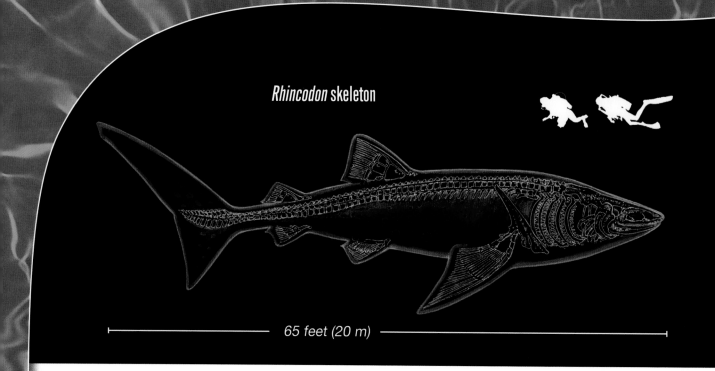

Rhincodon skeleton

65 feet (20 m)

still — literally, vertically upright! It has a special way of "sucking" into its massive mouth huge amounts of water, squirted past its "gill rakers." These bristly structures trap the small organisms on which it feeds.

Like ichthyosaurs did in the past, these particular sharks give birth to live young. One baby removed from its dead mother lived in captivity without eating for the first 17 days, even though it swam constantly. This shows that it had a lot of stored energy, probably in its very large, oily liver.

Rhincodon's fins and meat fetch a good price in many parts of the world. Perhaps because of too much hunting,

it is officially listed as an endangered species, one that might go extinct in our lifetimes. When something goes extinct, that means that the world has lost some of the incredibly intelligent programmed instructions that God put into the DNA of the many original kinds in those magnificent six days of creation, thousands of years ago. It seems much more tragic than losing the last copy of some ancient manuscript. Extinction is part of the relentless downhill process in biology that we see all around us. Genetic copying mistakes (mutations) are mostly scrambling information, never creating it, and extinction removes it forever. That sort of "bondage to decay," as Romans 8:21 puts it, can't go on forever, and the Bible tells us it won't (Romans 8:20–22; Isaiah 65:17; 2 Peter 3:13).

Some people have used the fact that *Rhincodon* has tiny teeth that are not used for biting to argue against the Genesis creation account. They say that God would not have made such "useless" structures, but how do we know they are useless? Many structures in the living world were once thought useless, and are now known to have a definite purpose.

The extinct *Leedsichthys*, another filter feeder, feasted upon plankton and krill.

Rhincodon teeth

Rhincodon also has tooth-like structures that extend onto its skin; the function of these was not known until recently, either. We now know that they help the shark move efficiently through the open ocean. The tiny "teeth" inside its mouth — there are 300 rows of them — may also make its filter feeding more efficient.

Just because we don't know the purpose of something does not mean there is no purpose; it means we don't know enough yet. For years, the human appendix was thought to be useless. It is now known to have an important function in the body's defense against disease, especially in childhood. Time and again, "useless" structures have been found to have a function after all, in defiance of evolutionary speculations.

Although *Rhincodon* has sometimes been seen in large groups, it generally prefers its own company, and is mostly found alone.

CRETOXYRHINA

Like all extinct sharks, with their skeletons of cartilage instead of bone, this brute did not leave many fossils behind other than its teeth. In the late 1800s, however, some remarkably complete specimens were found, suggesting that they had been rapidly buried.

Cretoxyrhina was about as large and heavy as the living great white shark, and quite similar in appearance. However, there are some differences, and we don't know if it was possibly a separate created kind.

The common name for this creature is the "Ginsu shark." This was named after the Ginsu knife, advertised on television with the catchy phrase: "It slices and dices," which is what *Cretoxyrhina* did. It used its incredibly sharp teeth to feed by "slicing" its victim up into bite-size pieces. We know that *Cretoxyrhina* even sliced into mosasaurs. A number of

Fast Facts

- Meaning of name: "chalk sharp-nose" (shark found in Cretaceous rock)
- Length: up to 25 feet (7 m)
- Weight: up to 3 tons
- "Discovered": 1843
- Location of fossils: United States
- Nifty fact: One rare, complete specimen containing 150 teeth was clearly flattened by the weight of the sediment that buried it.

specimens have been found of large pieces of partly digested mosasaur. Sometimes one finds *Cretoxyrhina* teeth still embedded in the victims. In one specimen containing two such teeth, two spinal bones had been bitten completely through, and there was evidence that the shark had swallowed and started digesting this portion of mosasaur.

We don't know, of course, to what extent such fossils resulted from scavenging of dead reptiles, rather than live attacks. The nature of the

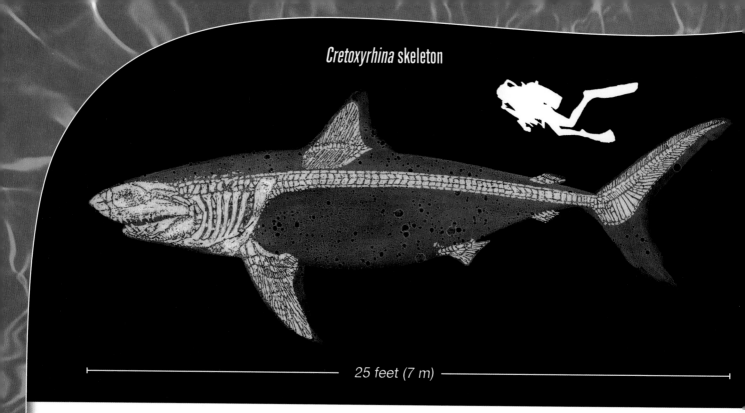

Cretoxyrhina skeleton

25 feet (7 m)

specimens suggests that at least some of them were "kill" bites. This must have been one deadly and powerful shark, to take on the beasts who were themselves regarded as having been magnificent predators of the sea. (Although if it tried to tackle the biggest *Mosasaurus*, long before it got to do any "slicing and dicing," it would probably be "crunched and munched" itself!)

In one specimen of a mosasaur, the evidence indicates that *Cretoxyrhina* attacked the creature and twisted its neck off. The violence of the attack left a broken tooth tip embedded in one of the mosasaur's bones. Most of the rib cage had been completely bitten through. There was evidence of subsequent scavenging, after *Cretoxyrhina* had had its fill, by a much smaller shark, also now extinct, named *Squalicorax*.

The evidence of these violent attacks, and particularly the scavenging afterward, reminds us that dead creatures don't lie on the sea floor quietly waiting to be buried by the slow, gentle accumulation of sediments over "millions of years." They would be sliced, diced, and "ripped apart" long before then! The particular mosasaur specimen described above still had strings of up to 14 vertebral bones in a row. If it had been sitting on

the sea floor even for months prior to being buried, the bones would have been much more scattered.

Also, there are many types of small organisms that start to decompose any bone that lies on the ocean floor. This is the reason why documentaries of the bottom of the ocean don't show hundreds of partially buried skeletons in the process of getting more fully buried over further eons of time. It simply doesn't

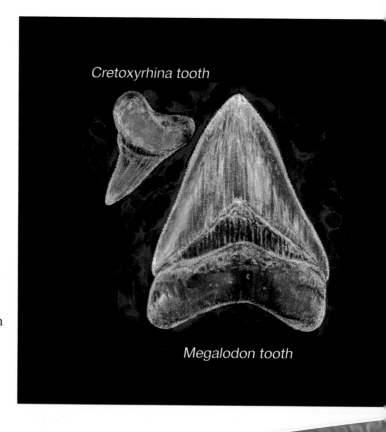

Cretoxyrhina tooth

Megalodon tooth

happen that way. Dead things on the bottom of the sea just don't stay intact and last for long. Even for skeletons to be preserved at all, they must be buried fairly soon, not hang around for "millions of years."

The specimen discussed above suggests that it was attacked, then scavenged, then at some point soon after this (days or weeks later — certainly not thousands of years, let alone millions) the scavenging process was interrupted because it was rapidly buried under sediment. I'm not saying that local catastrophes can't do this, but the "slow and gradual" theory about the formation of fossils is deeply ingrained in people's minds. It keeps on strengthening the "millions of years" belief system of our culture. One needs to think carefully about the whole issue of fossil formation. The presence of countless billions of rapidly buried fossils all over the world is strongly consistent with the Bible's record of the Genesis flood and the inevitable upheavals over the subsequent centuries.

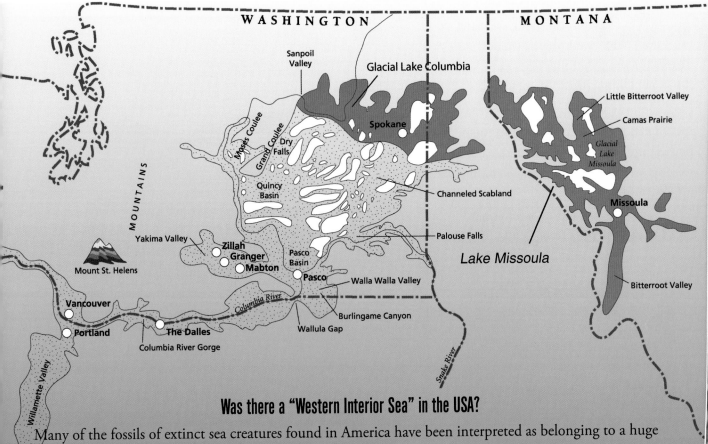

Was there a "Western Interior Sea" in the USA?

Many of the fossils of extinct sea creatures found in America have been interpreted as belonging to a huge inland sea that once covered large portions of what is now the United States.

This interpretation of the evidence is always presented within the erroneous "millions of years" belief system. Such beliefs put death and bloodshed before the fall of Adam, and they reject the clear history of the Bible.

But does that mean that the belief in such a sea having existed is definitely wrong? Not necessarily. There may well have been a large inland body of water left over after the Flood. There is evidence that Australia may once have had an inland sea as well, also post-Flood.

The fossils of the creatures that inhabited it may be the result of large regional upheavals after the Flood, aftershocks as the earth was settling down over centuries. Even many long-age scientists agree that it was a huge catastrophe in the northwest United States that carved the Channeled Scablands more or less in one big rush. A massive lake (Lake Missoula) formed from melting Ice Age glaciers broke its natural barriers.

BASILOSAURUS

too, *Basilosaurus* would have given birth to live young, underwater. Marine mammals like whales and dolphins also suckle their young with milk — underwater! Both of these processes require some spectacular and

Similar in many ways to the still-living creatures we know as whales, *Basilosaurus* was in other ways quite different. Unlike them, it had a very long, almost snake-like body. Its relatively small head meant that, despite its huge body length, it was probably restricted to feeding on modest-sized prey, including fish and squid.

It was, like the whales, a mammal, which breathed air via lungs. Like them,

Fast Facts

- Meaning of name: "king reptile"
- Length: 50 to 65 feet (15–20 m)
- Weight: 8 to 10 tons
- "Discovered": 1834
- Location of fossils: USA, Egypt, England
- Nifty fact: *Basilosaurus* did not use a blowhole, like whales do, to breathe air; it breathed through its nostrils, raising the tip of its nose out of the water.

very special design features to prevent the young from drowning.

Basilosaurus is thought to have had a tail fluke (a horizontal "flipper" that can move up and down), but wave-like motions (undulations) of its long, snaky body were probably the main way it generated the thrust it needed to swim and catch its food. At some 60 feet (18 m) long (imagine ten football players lying down end to end on a football field), it rivaled the huge, still-living sperm whale in length. Like the sperm whale,

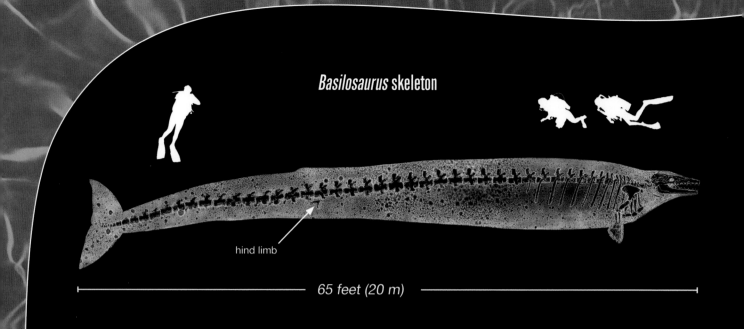

Basilosaurus skeleton

hind limb

65 feet (20 m)

its jaws contained teeth. But because it was so slender in comparison, it was less than a third as heavy. Even then, it still weighed as much as six to eight automobiles put together.

We saw earlier that, in times past, there have been many sailors' tales of encounters with "sea serpents." The descriptions of the body shapes vary, but, as the name suggests, they are generally much more snake-like than anything found today. With its serpentine shape, *Basilosaurus* is only one of a number of creatures we find as fossils that could have been responsible for some of these reports. Remember, most creatures that go extinct do not do so all at once; they tend to gradually decline in numbers, becoming ever rarer and more infrequently sighted.

Some scientists who promote the idea of evolution claim that the entire group in which *Basilosaurus* is classified was in-between modern whales and some imaginary ancestor from which they were supposed to have evolved. According to this view, this group (archeoceti) contains the ancestors of modern whales. However, other experts, even though they are still opposed to the Bible's account of creation, firmly reject the idea that the archeocetes are good candidates

Rear appendage

as "in-between forms." In fact, they were highly specialized creatures. There is no reason to think that they were in the process of evolving into anything else.

One particular skeleton of this creature, discovered in Egypt, was named *Basilosaurus isis,* after the Egyptian goddess Isis. If you look closely at drawings of its skeleton, or reconstructions of what it looked like, you can see that it had tiny hind limbs. At first this news generated great excitement among evolutionists. This is because they believe that whales came from creatures that used to walk on the land. So was this a whale that still had the legs it once used for walking? No, scientists discovered that the rear appendages of *Basilosaurus* were fully functional, not some useless leftover. They had working joints, with muscles attached, so they must still be used. But what for? Certainly not walking — they would not reach the "floor." They are so incredibly tiny in proportion to the rest of the body of the huge *Basilosaurus* that scientists generally agree that they could not even be used for paddling. It seems that they were most likely designed to be used as claspers in mating, just as one sees in some types of snakes.

In many ways similar to Basilosaurus, but about half its size, the marine mammal Zygorhiza (above) would have also been a formidable predator. The largest teeth (the second and third premolars) are 2 to 2½ inches (5 to 6 cm) wide in a fully-grown individual.

The fish drawn here are called Taimen Trout. Their fossils have been recovered from the same rocks as those of *Basilosaurus*. They are found living today in both freshwater lakes and rivers as well as the open ocean. Taimens are the largest member of the salmon family. *Basilosaurus* may have included them in its regular diet. Ferocious fighters, Taimen Trout are an angler's dream.

ARCHELON

Believe it or not, the spectacular variety of animals which were created to live in the sea includes turtles that were the size of VW Beetle autos! None of them are alive anymore, but *Archelon ischyros* was truly a giant of a turtle. It was 16 feet (5 m) from snout to tail, and about 13 feet (4 m) wide, flipper to flipper.

Many turtles have a shell consisting of tightly packed shell bones. However, *Archelon*'s shell was different from these.

The bony framework of its shell was probably covered in life with a series of horny plates, or else a leathery layer, like today's leatherback sea turtle. Some scientists actually think it may have been a larger relative of the leatherback turtle. So it could well have been descended from the same original Genesis (created) kind.

Fast Facts

- Meaning of name: "large turtle"
- Length: up to 16 feet (5 m)
- Weight: 5 tons or more
- "Discovered": 1895
- Location of fossils: mid-northern USA
- Nifty fact: The best-preserved specimen was found with its head bowed and "arms" folded, as if it were sleeping on the sea floor when it was suddenly buried in limestone.

Giant representatives of many created kinds have likewise not survived, even though the smaller types have. For example, we know that Australia's animal population included giant forms of kangaroos and emus in the fairly recent past. The ancestors of today's indigenous Australian people are known to have hunted these. This means that giant kangaroos and emus were still present when the first people arrived in Australia, after the Flood and the dispersion of people at Babel.

Archelon had a long, narrow head and a pointy tail. Its immensely powerful beak would have produced a phenomenal bite, even though it had no cutting edge

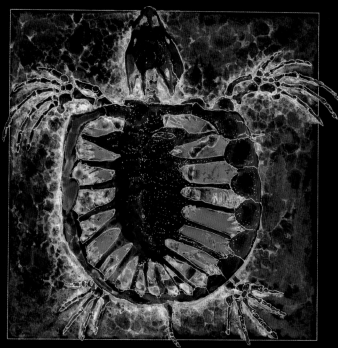

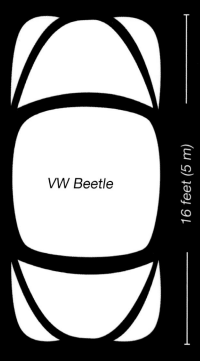

VW Beetle

16 feet (5 m)

like some beaked turtles have. The upper jawbone was hooked, with a large overhang or "overbite" similar to snapping turtles. Researchers have suggested that it may have used its beak not just for capturing and crushing its food, but perhaps digging for it as well. Many turtles, even if they have powerful jaws, are known to eat mostly jellyfish. That may have been a favorite food for *Archelon*, too, despite its impressive biting equipment.

Turtles today are regarded as among the world's most intelligent reptiles, and there is no reason to think *Archelon* would have been different in that respect.

All turtles lay their eggs on land, crossing beaches to dig their nests. Think of being on the beach on a quiet evening, back when some of these monster turtles were still alive. Then imagine you were to see this car-sized

colossus, a female *Archelon*, drag itself across the sandy strip in front of your eyes. No doubt, it would have kept a wary eye on you while excavating a home for its offspring-to-be. Of course, turtles are not known for speed, so *Archelon* would not have been an exception. Even knowing that, I think you would have kept a safe distance from her massive hooked beak!

Like other turtles, which are reptiles, *Archelon* breathed air. It therefore had to come to the surface at regular intervals. So, even though it was very large, people would have been able to sometimes kill the *Archelon* turtle in boats with spears and harpoons as it came up for air. What a feast that would have made for a whole village! Perhaps that is one reason why we don't find *Archelons* in the sea today.

No one has yet found an *Archelon* fossil with spearpoints or other evidence of human activity in it, but fossils in general only form rarely, in special conditions, and *Archelon* fossils are even rarer than most other fossils. However, we know from God's infallible record of history that people and *Archelon* must have lived on the same earth at the same time, just like its smaller cousins, the leatherback turtles, do today.

Leatherback turtles

Modern-day sea turtle

The first *Archelon* fossil find in modern times, in 1895, was by Dr. George Wieland, of Yale University. He was a well-known (in his day) fossil expert.

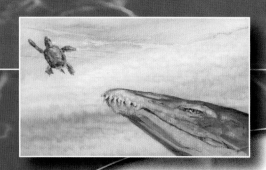

Ask someone, "What is the biggest and baddest predator that ever lived?" and often they will think of the mighty *Tyrannosaurus rex* (even though there is controversy about whether *T. rex* was actually a scavenger instead of a hunter). The title of "Biggest and Baddest" really belongs to a creature in the sea. It is probably a "draw" between *Liopleurodon* and *Kronosaurus*, whom we met on page 14. Both of these fearsome sea monsters are thought to have weighed nearly twice as much as the biggest meat-eating land dinosaur. (The mosasaurs we encountered earlier could grow bigger than both of these, but were probably not as fast and terrible.)

There is a lot of guesswork in paleontology (the science of fossils), so arguments rage over exactly how big *Liopleurodon* was. In fact, many books and Internet sources today say that it was about ten times as large

Fast Facts

- Meaning of name: "smooth-sided tooth"
- Length: 30–40 feet (9–12 m)
- Weight: 8–10 tons
- "Discovered": 1873
- Location of fossils: Europe
- Nifty fact: *Liopleurodon* could sample the water streaming through its nostrils in "stereo" to tell which direction smells came from.

as the measurements used in this book. They are probably deriving this information from the famous pro-evolution BBC series *Walking with Dinosaurs*. It featured *Liopleurodon* as being more than 80 feet long, and weighing 150 tons! Most fossil experts strongly disagree, however. The fairly complete skeletons of

Liopleurodon indicate that it was less than a third that size, so that is what this book will use. However, there may, in fact, have been a marine predator much larger than any that have been reliably reconstructed to date that would fit these seemingly exaggerated statistics. Tantalizing hints of this come from isolated scraps of

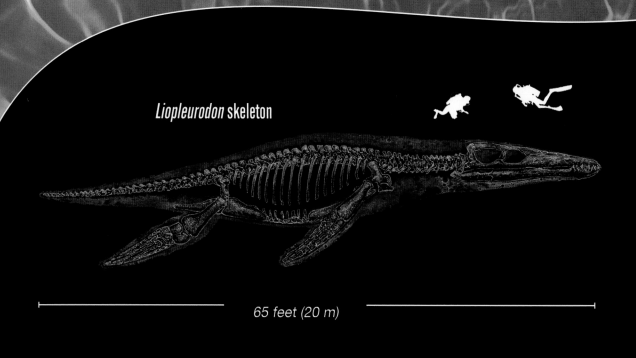

Liopleurodon skeleton

65 feet (20 m)

fossil bone, but these are never enough to be sure of what the original creature was like. It may even turn out that these larger pieces of bone really did come from some specimens of *Liopleurodon*, which actually reached such sizes. However, even at the most modest, conservative estimates (which have it weighing around ten tons), *Liopleurodon* was a powerful colossus of a carnivore.

When the question is asked, "What did it eat?" it's tempting to say, "Anything it wanted!" Its enormous ten-foot mouth was packed with very sharp teeth which were twice as long as those of *T. rex*. A favorite food seems to have been large squid. The evidences of its voracious appetite include half-eaten *ichthyosaurs* and teeth marks in the flippers of other large marine reptiles. It would have been capable of making a meal out of some of the larger sharks, too.

Liopleurodon was, like *Kronosaurus*, a pliosaur, a short-necked, large-headed type of marine reptile. It probably lay in wait to ambush its prey with huge bursts of speed, propelled by its large, powerful flippers.

We know from the Bible that *Liopleurodon* wasn't a passenger on the ark — no sea creatures were. It probably went extinct along with countless thousands of other types of marine animals, from the massive volcanic upheavals assosiated with the global Flood. Thinking of those savage jaws, maybe it's just as well!

Liopleurodon tooth

T. rex tooth

Science and the Past

A typical dig site at Grand Staircase-Escalante National Monument in southern Utah — the creature is probably something similar to Gryposaurus.

Why do we think we "know" that the teeth marks found in some fossil plesiosaur flippers came from *Liopleurodon*? Because the teeth of this creature are arranged in the front of its snout in a distinctive "rosette" fashion. So when we see that sort of bite pattern we can, like a crime investigator, reasonably deduce who the villain was.

The study of the past involves what is known as forensic (historical) science, but this has strong limitations, because we can't repeat the past, and we can't directly observe it. We can do repeatable experiments to find out how the world works (such as proving the law of gravity) with a high degree of certainty. However, we can't use testable, observable or repeatable scientific methods to try to prove things about the past.

If we start with God's record of history given in the Bible, we can make sense out of the facts relevant to that history, such as fossils. Those who start with a belief in evolution, rejecting the Bible, also have to interpret facts. Their starting point will make a big difference as to how they interpret them. For instance,

creationists assume that *Liopleurodon* descended from a created kind that looked a lot like it. However, they have never seen this original kind, and were not there at the creation. They rely on the "eyewitness" account in Genesis. Evolutionists assume that *Liopleurodon* evolved from something that didn't look anything like it. They were not there, either, and have never seen anything like this sort of revolutionary change happening. They might search among the many other fossil creatures for a possible "ancestor candidate," but no one could use experimental science or direct observation to show that *Liopleurodon* really did come from such a creature, even if it were found. In fact, it would merely be a separate created kind with some differences and similarities.

Science is a wonderful tool, but we need to be aware of the different sorts of science and their limitations. Beliefs and biases make all the difference in how facts are interpreted.

BALAENOPTERA
(THE BLUE WHALE)

container, and put it on truck scales, its blood would weigh ten tons! A small child could crawl through one of its major blood vessels. This whale can grow as long as seven automobiles parked end to end, and weigh as much as 35 African elephants!

Not all sea monsters were reptiles, or had massive, sharp teeth. The most monstrous of them all is still living in the sea today. *Balaenoptera musculus* is far and away the biggest creature God ever created, whether on sea or land. The blue whale, as it is more commonly called, is the biggest of the group of whales known as the *Balaenoptera*, or fin whales, which may have all descended from one created kind. It is much bigger than the largest dinosaur. Its tongue alone weighs more than an elephant, and is so big that 50 people could stand on it!

The blue whale's heart is about the size of a compact automobile, weighing more than half a ton. If one poured out all of the blood from its body into a

Fast Facts

- Meaning of name: "fin whale little mouse"
- Length: up to 100 feet (30 m)
- Weight: up to 200 tons
- "Discovered": 1758
- Location: all the world's oceans
- Nifty fact: The thrust of its tail alone can generate as much power as 500 galloping horses.

The blue whale is a record-breaker in other ways, too. It is the loudest animal on earth, with a whistle that can reach 188 decibels (dB). No wonder it can communicate in this way with other whales more than 500 miles away!

A blue whale migrates farther than any other mammal — up to 12,000 miles a year. It is also the fastest-growing creature on earth. Starting life as a microscopic embryo, when born one year later, it is about 25 feet (8 m) long and around 3 tons in weight.

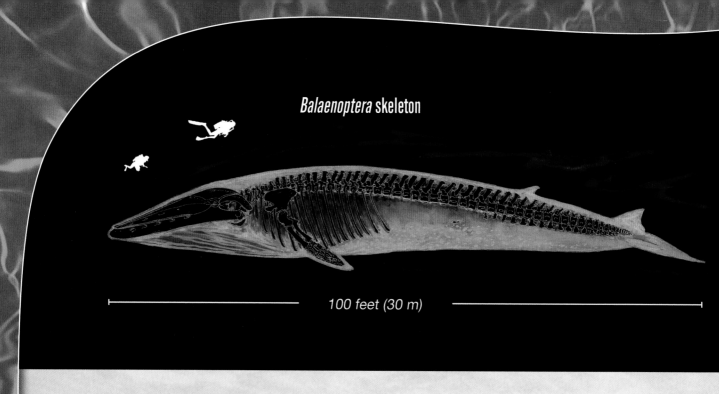

Balaenoptera skeleton

100 feet (30 m)

A blue whale calf can drink as much as 100 gallons (400 liters) of its mother's fat-rich milk every day. It gains weight at the rate of about 8 pounds (4 kg) an hour — some 200 pounds (91 kg) per day! It grows in length at about 1½ inches (4 cm) daily.

Despite its awesome size, the blue whale is harmless to people. The throat in its massive mouth is only a few inches in diameter. It uses huge comb-like plates to filter plankton and small shrimp-like organisms, called krill, from the sea. These plates are called baleen, or whalebone, but they are made of keratin, like that in our nails and hair, not bone at all. A blue whale needs to eat about four tons of food every day (its stomach can hold one ton), so it must filter very large volumes of water. It does this not just by using its forward motion through the water, but also by taking big "gulps" whenever its food is available in more concentrated amounts.

When the whale expels air and water at the surface, it is called a "blow" or "spout," which can reach 30 feet (9 m) high into the air, making it easy for whalers to spot.

In the days of hand harpoons and rowboats, it was nearly impossible to catch the powerful blue whale — when alarmed, it can swim as fast as 30 mph. It was only with later inventions, such as harpoons that could be fired from guns, that the mighty blues could be hunted and killed — sadly by the thousands. Now that hunting them is banned, their numbers are recovering, but at one time, their numbers may have dwindled to as low as only 500 in the whole world.

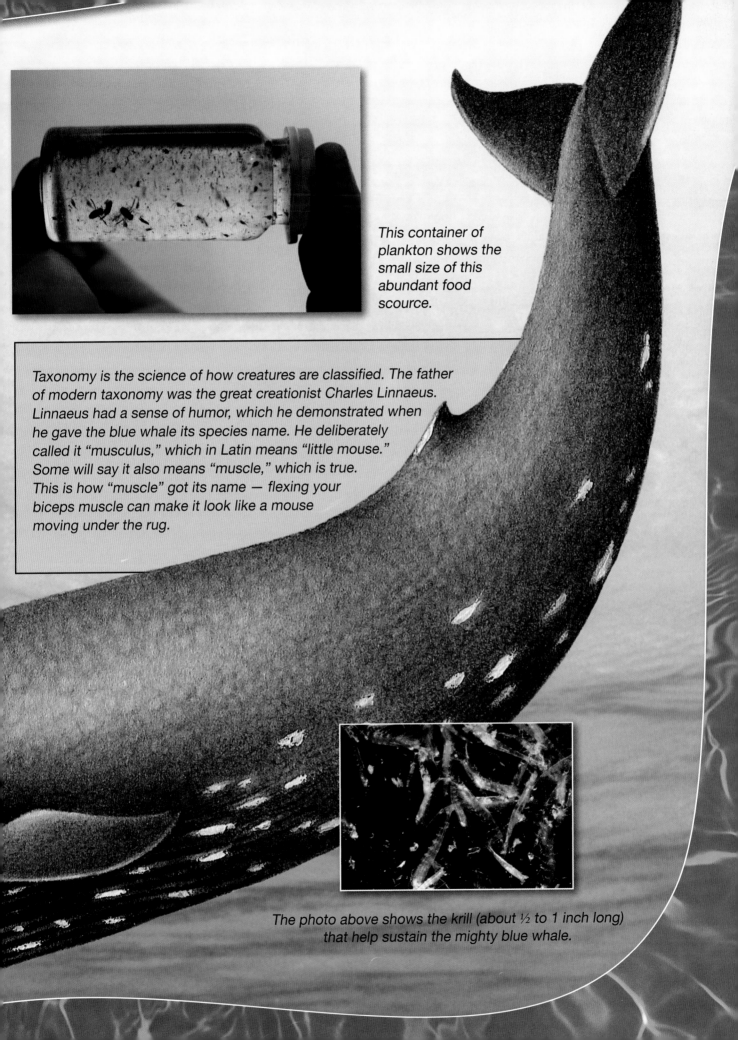

This container of plankton shows the small size of this abundant food scource.

Taxonomy is the science of how creatures are classified. The father of modern taxonomy was the great creationist Charles Linnaeus. Linnaeus had a sense of humor, which he demonstrated when he gave the blue whale its species name. He deliberately called it "musculus," which in Latin means "little mouse." Some will say it also means "muscle," which is true. This is how "muscle" got its name — flexing your biceps muscle can make it look like a mouse moving under the rug.

The photo above shows the krill (about ½ to 1 inch long) that help sustain the mighty blue whale.

DUNKLEOSTEUS

I f the movie *Jaws* had been made a few thousand years ago, this fish, and not the great white shark, might have been the movie's star.

Dunkleosteus (named after Dr. David Dunkle, who studied its bones) may have had the most powerful jaws of any living creature. It actually ate sharks for lunch!

Lacking actual teeth, it had two razor-sharp bony cutting blades instead. The edges of these sharp plates were serrated (like a saw). As they were worn down by use, new bone kept growing to regenerate them.

At up to 30 feet (9 m) in length (like five tall men end to end) and

weighing over a ton, *Dunkleosteus* would have been a fearsome predator. Its skull alone was over two feet long.

The powerful tail of *Dunkleosteus* was very much like that of a shark. It would have propelled itself forward by side-to-side movements of its body and tail. The body of *Dunkleosteus* was not covered in scales, but its head and chest region were protected by hinged body shields, which acted like very effective

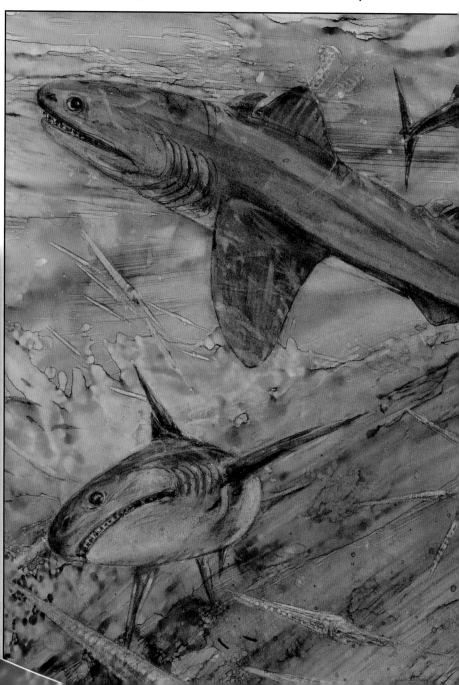

Fast Facts

- Meaning of name: "Dunkle's bones"
- Length: to 30 feet (9 m) or more
- Weight: up to one ton
- "Discovered": 1867
- Location of fossils: Morocco, Africa, Russia, Poland, Belgium, USA
- Nifty fact: As the sharp jaw blades of *Dunkleosteus* rubbed against each other, they kept themselves constantly sharp.

armor plating. These shields would have given it some protection against being eaten by other, also very powerful predators — some of whom we have met in the pages of this book.

The group in which it is classified is called the placoderms, or armored fishes. There are no placoderms known to be alive today. One can only speculate why this is so. But in fact we can tell from the fossils of buried fish that many fish types have become extinct since Noah's flood. Remember that Noah was not ordered to take any sea creatures on board. The Flood, with its breakup of the "fountains of the great deep" for five months, would have seen vast underwater earth movements and volcanic activity. This would have released many toxic chemicals over vast areas. In addition, the huge underwater mudslides we talked

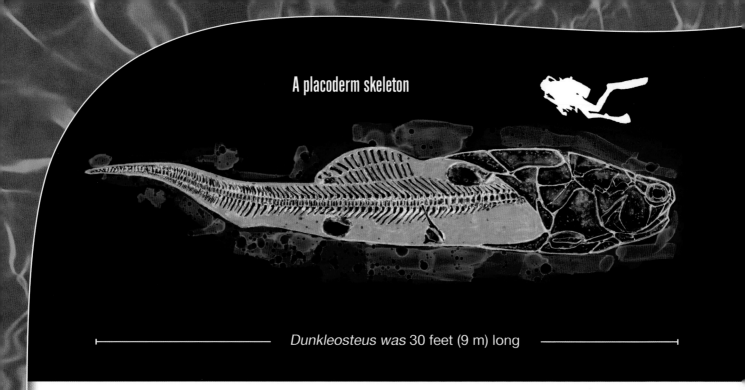

A placoderm skeleton

Dunkleosteus was 30 feet (9 m) long

about on page 20 would have buried billions of fish. The placoderms, with their heavy armor, may have been more vulnerable to being killed in this way.

Scientists have speculated that this fish must have suffered a lot of indigestion. This is because its fossils are often found with the remains of regurgitated, half-digested fish. But this might not be the case. Remember that both *Dunkleosteus* and those half-digested fish found next to it would not be preserved in a recognizable way unless they were quickly buried. *Dunkleosteus* may in fact have been regurgitating its food during its death throes, just as it was being buried in suffocating mud.

An armor-plated skull of Dunkleosteus

There's Design in the Curse

The original world before the Fall (Genesis 3) had no violence or suffering among the animals, which all ate plants (Genesis 1:29–31), although there are many structures in both fossil and living animals which would help creatures attack and eat others (or defend themselves against being eaten).

So what were such structures used for before the Fall? Physical features like sharp teeth, for instance, could have been used for other things pre-Fall. There is a bat with sharp teeth that eats fruit, and pandas strip and eat bamboo using the same sorts of teeth that other animals use for eating meat. We see much evidence, in sea creatures especially, of incredibly well-designed hunting and killing machines, and not just in regard to teeth by any means. Also, many structures seem brilliantly designed to protect creatures against being killed and eaten.

Panda

Thus, in many cases at least, God must have deliberately designed such equipment for a fallen world. Perhaps He reshuffled many genetic codes (the "programming of life") after the Fall. Or perhaps, knowing that it would not be long before Adam sinned, the Creator had all the instructions "in place," ready to be unleashed before long. Contemplating many of the more savage "dragons of the deep" certainly reminds us of the horrible nature of sin.

Remember, God had every right to judge the world for Adam's sin by introducing a temporary reign of death and bloodshed, which will be fully overcome in the future new heavens and new earth — because of the completed death, bloodshed, and resurrection of the Last Adam, Jesus Christ. Are you trusting Him so that you can be in that coming world forever?

Fruit Bat

Index

Photo Credits

Ardea, 36 (lower left)
Corbis, 21, 33 (main), 47, 62, 71 (upper left)
Courtesy of the Creation Adventures Museum
    Arcadia, Florida, Dr. and Mrs. Gary E. Parker,
    36 (lower right cutout)
Evangelos/Pangaea Fossils, 66 (lower left)
Francois Gohier/Ardea, 66 (lower right)
Getty, 70, 71 (lower), 75
Indiana, 9 Fossils, 17

Jaime Plaza Van Roon/Ardea, 38 (upper)
Nature Picture Library Ltd., 51
Nevada Commission on Tourism, 24
Pat Luthy/Imago Press, 26, 27
Pierre Jerlstrom (PhD)/AIG, 38 (lower photos)
Superstock, 33 (inset)
University of Michigan, 58
University of Oklahoma, 74

Our Customers' Favorite "Wonders of Creation" Book Series

Unearth the Special Features!

Each book includes over 200 beautiful four-color photos and illustrations, practical hands-on learning experiments, charts, graphs, glossary, and index — it's no wonder these titles never fail to be one of our most requested series. Students will enjoy the FREE pull-out color poster in the back of the book. The correlating study guides make them the perfect subject-intensive product. Order paperback study guides, or download them from our website for FREE!

- *The Archaeology Book* uncovers ancient history from alphabets to ziggurats.
- *The Cave Book* digs deep into the hidden wonders beneath the surface.
- *The Astronomy Book* soars through the solar system separating myth from fact.
- *The Geology Book* provides a tour of the earth's crust pointing out the beauty and the scientific evidences for creation.
- *The Fossil Book* explains everything about fossils while also demonstrating the shortcomings of the evolutionary theory.
- *The Ocean Book* explores the depths of the ocean to find the mysteries of the deep.
- *The Weather Book* delves into all weather phenomena, including historical weather events.

8 1/2 x 11 • Casebound • 96 pages • Four-color interior
ISBN-13: 978-0-89051-573-0 • $16.99 each
JR. HIGH to HIGH SCHOOL

ORDER PAPERBACK STUDY GUIDES $3.99 each

sample interior from The Ocean Book

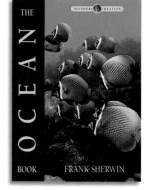

The Ocean Book
ISBN-13: 978-0-89051-401-6

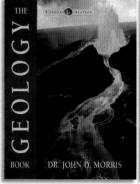

The Geology Book
ISBN-13: 978-0-89051-281-4

The Weather Book
ISBN-13: 978-0-89051-211-1

The Astronomy Book
ISBN-13: 978-0-89051-250-0

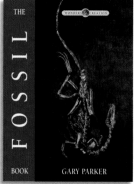

The Fossil Book
ISBN-13: 978-0-89051-438-2

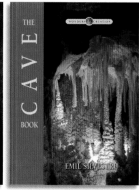

The Cave Book
ISBN-13: 978-0-89051-496-2

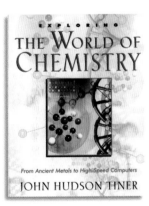

EXPLORING
THE WORLD OF
BIOLOGY

From Mushrooms to Complex Life Forms

JOHN HUDSON TINER

8-1/2 x 11 Paperback • 160 pages • b&w interior
ISBN-13: 978-0-89051-552-5 • $13.99 each

The Top-selling "Exploring" Series

A great evolution-free resource tool!

This series provides a solid foundation of fact for each subject. Concise information, along with chapter questions, illustrations, and photos to emphasize the facts builds a strong foundation for understanding their respective topic from a Christian world view. Each book includes over 100 illustrations, charts, and photos along with key facts, terms, definitions, chapter review questions, and answer key.

- *Exploring the World of Biology* From Mushrooms to Complex Life Forms.
- *Exploring Planet Earth* uncovers the history of civilization, historical people, and places.
- *Exploring the History of Medicine* examines modern medicine from ancient Greeks to today.
- *Exploring the World Around You* tours the planet and its seven biomes.
- *Exploring the World of Mathematics* traces the history of mathematic principles and theories.
- *Exploring the World of Physics* captures the workings of simple machines to nuclear energy.
- *Exploring the World of Chemistry* investigates ancient metals to high-speed computers.

A topic-specific, information-rich, evolution-free series from Master Books

The World of Chemistry
ISBN-13: 978-0-89051-295-1

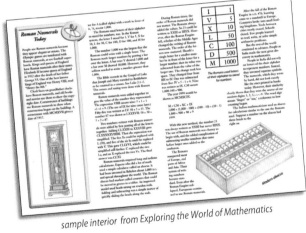

sample interior from Exploring the World of Mathematics

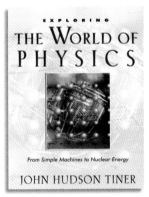

The World of Physics
ISBN-13: 978-0-89051-466-5

The World Around You
ISBN-13: 978-0-89051-377-4

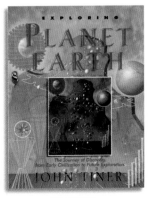

The World of Mathematics
ISBN-13: 978-0-89051-412-2

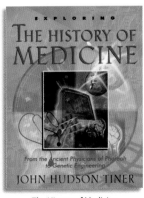

Planet Earth
ISBN-13: 978-0-89051-178-7

The History of Medicine
ISBN-13: 978-0-89051-248-7